THE CHIEF X OFFICER

A Survival Guide for Turbulent Times

THE SURVIVAL GUIDE FOR CHANGE AGENTS • WHAT TO DO IN THE FIRST NINETY DAYS THAT WILL DECIDE YOUR FUTURE WITH THE ORGANIZATION • WHAT IT TAKES TO SUCCEED IN MIDDLE AND SENIOR MANAGEMENT IN A COMPANY THAT IS EXPERIENCING TRANSFORMATION • A MUST-READ FOR ANYONE WANTING TO EXCEL AS A CORPORATE CHANGE AGENT

Majed A. Rahim and Basil A. Nabi

ISBN: 1-4392-6058-3
ISBN-13: 9781439260586

Visit www.booksurge.com to order additional copies.

Contents

Foreword

This book is a quick guide for executives joining a new organization, replacing a long tenured predecessor or filling a newly created post, and intending to turn things around by bringing new ideas, creativity, experiences and energy to places where stagnation or dysfunction has ruled for some time. Now that the interviews are done, your contract negotiated, notice period served, today is the first day on the job. Now what? This book walks you through what to expect in the first few hours and months, shows you how to quiet the doubts, quell the challenging regard of the cynics, and show quick results.

These chapters are based on personal experiences and great feedback from friends, colleagues, peers, bosses, subordinates, and customers.

"Three months of running a business or trying to set up a business and you will learn, I suspect, as much as you can learn in three years at a business school."

Richard Branson

While there are no "silver bullets" when it comes to turning things around (we dedicate a whole chapter to this), going back to basics is the closest you will get to ensuring success.

If, like us, you like to pick up books and guides to help you as a manager, and like to skim through them on a plane or train ride, we think you will enjoy this book. We try to avoid pontificating (as much as we can), and stay away from stock advice and worn out clichés. Not to disappoint you, but the word "paradigm" does not appear in this book except in this Foreword.

This book is meant to be read in 30-60 minutes, and it's chapters can be read out of sequence without affecting its flow; after all, how many times do you start your day with a neatly written "to-do" list and by 4:00 pm find out that you managed to scratch off one item, and added five more.

We hope you will enjoy reading and applying the lessons learned in these chapters, and that they will add some insight and spice to your new role.

⌘ ⌘ ⌘

Introduction

Throughout our careers, we have had the mixed pleasure or displeasure of taking over other peoples' jobs, staff, responsibilities, headaches, bosses, and customers. Like you, after a long and exhaustive search we were selected and tasked to shape things up, turn the ship around, polish off the old brass, and squeeze 110% out of our groups. We heard all these tired clichés that organization leaders like CEOs and Chairpersons like to throw at new senior managers with the hope that they will be inspired, and take charge.

Reality could not be farther from these empty words.

Most of us like to be told that we "got the right stuff" and that our predecessors were asleep at the wheel; that we possess skills and talents that are unique and hard to find, and that from this reservoir of experiences and battle scars we can turn any organization around. Moreover, they are right. We can do it. However, we cannot do it by the click of a mouse; we cannot do it via email, and we cannot do it alone.

Today is the first day, its 8:15 a.m., and you are waiting for the Sponsor (or Director) to show up while sitting across from his secretary in the waiting room. You made it a point of showing up 15 minutes early (must make that first good impression), put on the right suit (not the one you wore for the last interview), your briefcase by your polished shoes. All the while you are sizing up the secretary, trying to decide if she is going to be helpful in letting you reach the Sponsor when you need to, or if she is just a nicely dressed and carefully made up pain the neck.

At this point, you are probably getting a couple of text messages on your phone from your significant other, wishing you well on your first day, asking you to keep them updated throughout the day, and letting you know how proud of you they are. All the while, the new shoes are starting to hurt your heels, and where the heck is the Sponsor?

If this sounds familiar, well, join the club. No matter how senior we get, and how fancy our titles are, this hellish wait for the boss to show up, the brief meeting and strained chitchat (since you are after all fixing problems that happened on his/her watch), and then the elevator ride to your floor and your new office will give the most accomplished career executive a case of heartburn. This is perfectly normal. After all, you did leave your last job because you wanted to do something else; you have years and years of proven experience, and the Sponsor was so impressed with you they gave you this amazing job. Calm down, take a deep breath, send back a message to your significant other, and try to ignore the frosty looks you are getting from the secretary.

Finally, the Sponsor shows up in a huff. You sit across from him (no more sitting in front of the desk, that was for the interview only!), and then he/she gives you some pearls of wisdom for your first few days. More likely it will go something like this "Well, Bob/Barb, I'm happy you are finally on board! We have so much to do, the group/division/branch has been neglected for so long, and I am glad we finally have the right leadership to make things happen. You have my full support on any changes you need to make, and I am sure you will find your way very easily. For the next few days/weeks/months I will try (*keyword try*) to stay out of your way and give you all the space you need (*translation zero support, keeping a safe distance from the upcoming battle*) to come up with your own impressions, ideas, and plans (*they better match what I have in mind*), and then I look forward to seeing you as often as possible (once a week at best), and to observing improvements in due course (*by next week latest*). You have a good team under you (*losers*), and I am sure they will all give you all the support you require (*lucky if they don't spit in your coffee*). I don't want to prejudice your view (*but I will anyway*); Clark is an idiot, Chris is a lightweight, Sam is my pet employee, and John should have been fired eons ago, but I could not do it because I wanted the new leadership to assess the situation first (*read: I don't have the stomach for it, and I want you to do it*)".

Now you might think we are being too cynical, but we assure you we are not exaggerating. Now, let us think about this rationally.

Why were you hired in the first place? This is a multiple-choice question:

(A): The Sponsor is new, and needs someone to help him/her make a change quickly, i.e. does not trust or think highly of the existing executive team;

(B): The incumbent (your predecessor) was fired, and none of the existing line managers can/want to step up and take on the job;

(C): The incumbent retired after 30 years on the job, the last five of which were dedicated to maintaining business-as-usual;

(D): The Board, consultants, rating agency, auditors, regulators, etc. highlighted serious issues in the company's structure and the Sponsor needed to bring in fresh talent to close these gaping holes.

We have had the pleasure and misfortune of being recruited under each one of the four scenarios above. In addition, let us assure you that the result is the same, and the track to success is the same as well.

If you, our dear reader, assume that you can count on the Sponsor, or others to guide you or aid you, then unfortunately you will set yourself up for a major case of disappointment and disillusionment. Nobody likes the new guy with the fancy title, fat package, and sharp eye for improvement, sometimes least of all the Sponsor. So tread carefully.

Now comes the walk of fame. The Sponsor or a designated functionary will now take you around to introduce you to your peers, subordinates, and "make you feel at home", because that's what we do in this organization, We are, after all, a small family of 40,000 people in 6 countries and zillion offices. What we do not understand is that why they did not just let you drop off your briefcase first? Therefore, here you are walking down the hallways with your chaperon, shaking hands, introducing yourself. There is a hush on the floor, people are hanging up their phones, and poking their heads out of their dungeons to see the "new guy/gal", Compared to the wait in the Sponsor's outer office, this has to be our least favorite part of the first day. Do not get us wrong; we are people-oriented, and we really like to meet new people. Nevertheless, this forced and contrived way of meeting people is just torture.

You finally make it to your office. Luckily, the IT team has your computer set up, your email account is ready, and they were kind enough to give you a directory of internal extensions. In addition, a welcome package of new stationary. Come on, how can you conquer the world without a fresh supply of post-it notes, pencils (who uses those anymore), a desk calendar (hello, anyone hear of Outlook?), and a stapler.

You close the door, take a deep breath, and start exploring the office. Invariably, within 5 minutes, someone you met on your walk through pops his/her head in to welcome you again, and asks if you need anything. Take our advice, discount this person (more on that later).

Unless you are moving into a brand new office or building, there is a good chance you will find the following as you go through desk and cabinet drawers: old stationary, old business cards, some hanging folders, an older list of extensions, and some coin change. Moreover, we agree nothing can be more depressing that seeing the debris of someone else's career on your first hour on the job. This old stationary is bad for your mental health, and our advice is to throw it out immediately. Do not let the old ghosts haunt your new digs; this is your office, your world, and you need to shape it your way. Even changing the orientation of your office will make a difference, and will send a message of change, and of new things to come.

⌘　⌘　⌘

The Book Plan

This book has three distinct parts that build on each other, and which provide the reader with a complete guide for his/her journey of change empowerment in his/her new executive role.

- In Part I of the book, we focus on guiding the CxO's first few hours and days in the organization, to the initial meeting with your peers and team members.

- In Part II, we provide you with insights on how to navigate through the corporate culture, how to manage your relationships with your sponsor and peers, and how to survive and thrive in a less than ideal organizational setup.

- In Part III, we explain and give samples of simple yet rapid and effective tools that you, our reader, can readily and easily adapt and implement to accelerate your progress and to achieve your mission.

⌘ ⌘ ⌘

Part – I

Encounters

1. Meeting the troops

With the first couple of hours behind you, and the company email figured out, your office exorcised of old stationery and previous owner's belongings, it is now time to meet the troops.

Now, here is where things can vary from one setup to another. In some cases, during the interview process, you probably met some of the people who will work under you, to get a better feel for the place; this is likely if you joined because of scenario (C) above. However, under the other scenarios, chances are this will be the first time you come face to face with the "team" that you are now responsible for, and charged with leading, changing, overhauling, etc.

Not to scare you, but the careers of many executive 'CxOs' are made or destroyed in this meeting. So be very careful.

Now, before you consider holding this meeting, ask yourself why do you need to meet so soon? Does it have to be today? Will you really connect with these people in a forced, sterile environment of the meeting room? Unless you can emphatically answer "yes" to all these questions, our advice is to postpone this meeting for a couple of days.

A few tricks that worked for us in the past;

- Do your own walk through. Just get up, leave your suit jacket behind, and start popping into people's offices or cubicles. We cannot tell you how effective this technique is for breaking the ice, and getting people to feel more at ease. Here you are, the new boss, the one with the mandate to whip this place in shape, popping in to shoot the breeze with your team, no scheduled meetings, no summons to your office. You engage in a natural, easygoing dialogue that has nothing to do with work. Pick your first target at random and just plop yourself in front of him/her and talk and-- more --let them talk about any subject they feel comfortable without forcing an agenda, and do not interrupt. We can't emphasize enough how useful and effective this will be for your rapport and relationships with your team. During these meetings, keep your ears and eyes wide open, verbal and non-verbal queues will tell you more about these individuals than a million emails, interoffice memos or gossip. We're not saying that you should form an opinion or judge any person at this point; nothing is more dangerous than the 'I can figure people out in 30 seconds' mantra that some executives keep repeating. This is hogwash, pure and simple. People are complex, easily threatened, and multi-layered; do not think you can figure them out in one meeting. What you want to accomplish today is simply to break the ice, and show your human side.

- Try to see as many of the key people as you can on you first day. Chances are you will need a second day to see the whole team. No worries, tell the people you see the second day that there was no preconceived or planned sequence or order on the basis of which you selected those with whom you met the day before. This will put them at ease. They will also be more open and en-gaged as they have been hearing from the others how approachable and open you are.

- Once you complete the circle, start it again. Why? If you do not, then you will be wasting the entire effort, and will lose the goodwill you have been building. This time, mix in some work questions, and seek their advice. Nothing is more flattering or empowering than a new boss who genuinely wants your opinion or advice and seeks your council.

When you finish these informal meetings, get ready to hold the first staff/line managers meeting. Here again, there a few tips that worked for us, and we are confident you will find them useful:

- If there's a pre-scheduled meeting time and place from the previous administration, disregard it and schedule a new meeting schedule--a different day and time;
- Invite people yourself for the first meeting, either by another pop in, or on the phone. Save the Calendar Invitations till later; they're too impersonal at this stage;
- You do not need an agenda for the first meeting. Heck, you are lucky to find the conference room;
- Open by welcoming everyone, expressing your joy and excitement about being with them (and mean it), and then reiterate that this is an informal meeting;
- Start a round-robin dialogue; whenever someone is shy, or reluctant to open up (you don't know what these meetings were like before), nudge them, encourage and facilitate the meeting, and before you know it they will all be talking, and bringing up people, ideas, and feeling at ease;
- Keep a sharp eye for snipers, ambushers, and whiners (more on that later).

Keep the meeting to an hour, wrap up gently, thank everyone for his or her time, and set the time for the next meeting. Nominate a scribe and agree on a set agenda.

At this point, you should be a bit more comfortable with the team, and they should be more comfortable with you. You have interacted with them in both an informal and a semi-formal setting, and started on your journey on the right foot.

You can also be sure that word of these meetings will have gotten back to your Sponsor, as even the most aloof, above it all Sponsor will have his/her network of informants. The Sponsor should feel comfortable that you are reaching out to your team, and showing the signs of a man/woman of action.

⌘　⌘　⌘

2. Expanding the Circle

Now that you are on your way to getting to know your team, it is critical that you start looking outside your own domain and reach out to your peers.

This is another one of those dances that you need to master, and quickly. Most of us have run into peers who are supportive, creative, and just great people to work with; and most of us have run into peers who are jealous, petty, and a nightmare co-exist with. Chances are you will have both in your organization.

The unscheduled pop-in meeting will not work here. Either it will be seen as an interruption, taking liberties too soon, or you will be labeled as over-eager. What we found worked effectively is a combination: pick up the phone and start calling your peers, if you have not met them to date, introduce yourself, and offer to come up/down for a quick cup of coffee when their schedules allow. If you have already met, offer the same, and just pick up the thread of the conversation, no matter how superficial it is at this point.

Something worth keeping in mind is that some of these peers probably had strong ties (good, bad, or ugly) with your predecessor, and that is why it is vital to stay neutral, and listen more than you talk. Some might have tried for your job and did not get it, while some might have had your job, or similar jobs in other parts of your organization in the past. Again, be careful not to over-praise or criticize the company or your team now. Invariably, some of your team members will have stronger relationships with your peers, from shared history, or previous reporting relationships or both. Keep your opinions to yourself; you can destroy a budding relationship very fast by praising a peer who, in the past, made a habit of dressing down one of your line managers, or criticizing a peer who in the past had helped build the career of and/or hired that same line manager.

You have not had enough time to form opinions no matter how glaring the signs are, so avoid opining, keep your ears and eyes wide open, and do not fall into this trap.

Another good approach to help peers open up and be supportive is to simply ask them what they would like to see more/less of or introduced from your group. It is very easy to assume that we each manage separate organizational units with little or no interaction or dependency on other groups within the organization, but we could not be more wrong. Whether you are in a revenue generating line (i.e. sales driven) or a cost line (i.e. support function), we all cross paths both visible and invisible.

By simply reaching out in the most genuine and constructive way possible and asking your peers what their needs are, you will be forging constructive relationships and coming a step closer to your mission of making change happen at all levels.

There are people who will say (and we've been told that to our faces) that reaching out to one's team members and peers early in the game and seeking their thoughts and opinions undermines your authority and standing as the new chief, and that opening up to these "strangers" so quickly gives the impression that you are a lightweight who seeks validation or worse, a clueless hack who needs others to show him/her the way. That is the tough choice. Do you want to be an open and reachable executive and work with the group dynamics of the organization, and then lead the change from within, or a hard-charging axe-wielding warrior? We have tried both, and succeeded at both. However, if you want long lasting results that will stand the test of time and of changes at the top, we advise you to consider opening up, reaching out, and fixing the problem inside-out rather than outside-in.

It is also important to ask yourself a few more questions: do you really want to be <u>feared</u> or to be <u>respected</u>? Are you willing to put up with the fuzziness of the induction period? Do you have the stamina and the thick skin to withstand the criticism and the naysayers? What if your commander in chief calls you to tell that you are too soft and that you have not chopped enough heads after 72 hours on the job (true story!).

As accomplished but newly appointed managers, most of us have left behind careers where we shone and no longer needed to prove our worth. We also left behind a comfort zone where we knew everyone and everyone knew us or of us. Now, with a fancy title and a broad mandate, we are the new kid in class. Part of us wants the love and adoration and another part wants to show these simpletons that we are more qualified and better than anyone they have. Do not fall into this trap. Keep your ego and insecurities in check. Bite your tongue, reach out and build relationships from scratch, be open, and prepare yourself for the battle scars if they happen. At the end of the day, it will all be worth it.

<u>This is how we used to do it</u>

What a busy few days it has been. After the initial few hours of staring at the walls in your office, playing with your new computer, downloading some of your old data, and trying to organize your office to look more like you, it's time to get down to business.

By now, you have met your team and got a condensed idea of what they are doing, the issues they are facing, and most likely created a mental punch list of things you see as candidates for immediate correction. You have also opened yourself up to your colleagues, started to build bridges, and have some idea of how your group looks to others. Well, crack your knuckles and get ready for some serious change.

You are also comparing what you've gleaned over the last few days with what you are used to or helped create in the past, and can't believe some of the 'nonsense' that's been happening around here. You are also thinking to yourself, "This is

An example of taking previous experiences and practices and blindly assuming they will work in all scenarios is a manufacturer of heavy equipment we worked with on a large-scale technology project. The entire change program revolved around the need to automate and simplify the work environment to cut costs and shorten delivery cycles. The change mandate got off to a great start with an approved blueprint and a strong team in place. The first sign of trouble was when the management consultants hired to facilitate the process attempted to force a decision-making process where decisions and approvals are secured in 3 working days or less, and in writing. This clashed with a corporate culture that encouraged consensus and avoided conflict. While this culture was one of the impediments to achieving the goals of the change mandate, by attacking this culture outright and forcing a major cultural shift before the change mandate had put down its roots was a major mistake of the consulting team. The good intentions behind this change in process and culture did not save the change mandate from halting. Subsequently, a revised set of rules that changed existing practices and corporate culture was gradually introduced, but the change mandate suffered a delay and a black eye that could have been avoided by using a more skillful approach.

not going to be so hard, in a couple of weeks I will leave my print all over this place." You have also foolishly shared some of your observations with your Sponsor who—earlier discussion notwithstanding—is eager and curious to know what a super starter like yourself thinks of his shop, and wants to see results. Let us get to it.

STOP!!!!

You are exhibiting one of the classic symptoms of the most hated new executive, and sadly, the most common one. In your eagerness to show results and crawl back in your comfort zone, you fall back on all the experiences you have had, previous successes, and tools you have used before. While they make up your toolkit, you must pause and consider if they are compatible with the new environment.

Nobody likes the executive that sits in a meeting and keeps telling others (no matter how well intentioned), "I can't believe you are still doing such and such this way; in my old company we did this another way years ago."

Real life example: In a meeting with a fellow executive, the new guy droned on about how paper-intensive a certain function in the company is, and how in his previous place of work, automated workflow and document management systems have been in place for years. On the surface, it is a valid point. What the new person failed to understand is that the process he was criticizing involved just two people sitting in the same office and no more than 10 transactions a day, compared to a small army of people who did this at his previous place of business, due to the nature and volumes of the work. The observation was correct, the context was very wrong. You can take this simple example and extend it to numerous similarly simplistic assumptions, i.e. the recruiting system is wrong; the sales people are too well paid; we are over or understaffed; where's the video conferencing room; our old email system is better; we outsourced this function; we merged these functions, etc. Valid points, yes, but again, think of the context. We are not suggesting that we ignore what we know or have learned in the past. On the contrary, at the heart of it, this collection of tools, experiences, and insights is why we got the nod in the first place. What we are advising is that before we start parting with these pearls of wisdom that we take the necessary time to understand our new environments, put them in context, and most importantly, deliver them in the right way.

How to deliver or suggest these changes? We are burning with the desire to start making changes, but we would be foolhardy to start swinging away without first building the right platform.

Here are some practical steps that we learned the hard way:

1. Consider the audience: were the people around the table involved in these archaic practices? If they were, then you need to praise them for what they were able to do with few resources, and then gently introduce the new ideas, while refraining from referring to your old company, as that will just make them defensive. If asked or pressed on whether this has worked in the past, then you can reference your old successes.

2. If these practices are generally accepted as old and obsolete, you still need to proceed carefully, as some of the people around the table might have attempted in the past to make changes and failed, and will be quick to shoot down your ideas. Bring them to your side by

highlighting the track record of the new practices, and how you need all their support for this one to stick.

At the end of the day, what are we trying to accomplish? Is it to impress people with our ideas, and remind them that we worked in bigger, better, and more sophisticated places? Or simply deliver solid results and make the right changes? Newsflash: by now, everyone knows where we worked before. Some might be impressed, and others might be silently resentful. Constantly reminding them about it and showcasing our previous successes and best practices will backfire and have the opposite effect.

In brief, your tried and tested practices, insights, shortcuts, etc. are very valuable, but should be deployed in the right context, and with tactful delivery.

Summary: Expanding your circle of friends, allies, and colleagues is crucial; reaching out with care is needed, and remember, these people have been in the organization much longer than you have. Keep your hastily-formed opinions to yourself.

⌘ ⌘ ⌘

Part – II
Navigation

3. Back to Basics

What holds true for a professional athlete also holds true for a professional CxO: whenever in doubt, go back to the basics. In this chapter, we will attempt to explain these basics and how to call on this invaluable reservoir of experiences and practices acquired over many years of practice.

In the role of the designated CxO, we walk into organizations that are in dire need of change, and we are treated as either saviors or villains depending on the other person's perspective. As we discussed in the "This is how we used to do it" section, in our desire to effect change and to quell doubts, we overlook the basics of our craft.

Once we have had our observation period, gotten to understand the organization better, and built a team around us (a fragile alliance at this point), we need to roll up our sleeves and get to work. Our advice is to avoid all the fancy, complex, showy practices, and get back to the basics. Let us start by asking ourselves, and writing down the answers, to the following questions:

- How can I simplify the work of people around me?
- How can I separate the real problems from the emotions?
- What language or techniques can I use to reach and connect with the widest audience?
- How can I get more people to see the right way forward?
- How can I show results quickly? (An entire chapter is dedicated to this.)

"An example is an organization that had a call center which suffered from chronic problems; When the call center was established years ago, it was a dumping ground for mediocre and troubled employees, who rather than being counseled up or out, were shifted to a place where they didn't have face to face contact with customers (big mistake); Over the years, and to the amazement of everyone, that staff had actually turned themselves around and started delivering quality service. However, whenever they asked for additional investments in people or technology, their requests were turned down because the management of the organization still viewed the group as 'that center over there where all the trouble makers were relocated'. Going back to the basics, allowed the change agent to objectively examine the fundamentals of the call center and the industry approved metrics and prove to the organization's management that the center is performing and their requests are very much justified. To break through this wall of resistance built up over the years by emotions and perceptions meant going back to the basics, as no amount of pleading their case would have worked otherwise. Go back to the basics."

Start by avoiding complex, academic theories and approaches. An example is that of an organization we worked with that was suffering from a long and drawn out annual planning cycle and suffocated by a Sponsor who wanted to implement a Balanced Score Card approach in great minutia, which resulted in the top team abandoning the process and sabotaging it (and who can blame them?). After spending weeks in endless meetings arguing and trying to find the right words to express the goals and mission of the organization with a focus on slick, catchy phrases that aren't understood by the rest of the organization, going back to the basics meant examining the motives behind this planning process. At the core of it, the organization needed a set of goals, objectives, and targets that could guide its activities for the next 12-24 months. The academic aspect of the process was simply killing it. After rounds of discussion, the process was short-circuited to each business line manager coming up with a 3-page business plan that highlighted the targets and goals of his/her unit, holding themselves account-able for achieving these goals, and communicating them to the rest of the organization in the way they see fit. This resulted in clear and straightforward goals that everyone could relate to and work with rather than ambiguous and fancy-sounding state-ments that nobody could understand. Go back to the basics.

Focusing on the basics of the problem or task ahead can also mean neutralizing the history and baggage that we bring with us as we are attempting to make changes.

"Another example is of a major committee that reported to the board that it chronically fell behind on its objectives, to the disappointment of the committee's chairperson and the CEO. When examining the issue, it became apparent that what was causing the committee to always turn in its work behind schedule was the obsession of the committee scribe with drafting the meeting minutes and action items in the most elaborate and substantial form possible, without reviewing prior task commitments. This resulted in days of drafting, editing, and redrafting, while the issues went unresolved, and timelines slipped by. What the change agent did in this example was to first discuss the issue with the CEO and agree on a very concise and simple format for capturing the essence of the meeting and ensuing action items. This was provided to all committee members and the scribe with the mandate of issuing the document no later than 24 hours after the meeting, including prior actions' status. Rather than squabbling about the format and prose of the minutes, the group was able to focus on getting issues resolved and actions taken. Go back to the basics."

Another effective technique is to simplify the language when you find that the root of the problem is a lack of common language among the group.

One of our goals as CxOs is to reach the widest audience possible and engage the organization at all levels. If we keep in mind that the people we will deal with, as newcomers to the organization, have varying backgrounds and access to the latest in management theories and industry best practices, then the issue becomes clearer. How many long-serving staff members have not been on an external training course or seminar? In addition, how many were 'hidden' away from the latest wave of management consultants? Now, let us ask ourselves how will these same staff members (whom we will need and rely on) react to a fast talking, jargon spewing CxO? We would hazard that it will be a cold reception. If we stick to the basics of the job, strip away all the fancy packaging, and repackage our change initiative in simple, easy to relate to, and relevant practices and techniques, then we exponentially increase our chances of effecting the desired changes. This statement should NOT be construed as a way to dumb down the message. On the contrary, a shop floor worker is more likely to catch on to your message on the way to fix a supplier problem if presented in a clear, concise and pragmatic style.

In a later chapter, we discuss how to show results quickly by identifying the low hanging fruit. What we are outlining here is the credibility we want to establish rapidly. Going back to the basics means realizing that as humans (normal ones anyway), we have a natural mistrust of the CxO. If we hide behind theories and build elaborate change plans that take an eternity to produce results, we will lose the support of the people we need the most. Going back to the basics means that no suggested improvement is discarded because it is not fancy or slick enough, and no opportunity to clear away the fog is wasted in the pursuit of theory.

⌘ ⌘ ⌘

4. Understanding the Lay of the Land

Getting a good and fast grasp of the organization you have just joined and charged with turning around is an important skill (and task) that all new executives and CxOs need to develop and hone quickly.

While it is true that no two organizations are the same, more often than not, we operate and are in charge of organizations that have many similarities.

In our capacities as czars of change and the new executives on the block, the sooner we understand the intricacies of our new home, the sooner we will be able to deploy our tools of change. I am not talking about where the cafeteria and the bathrooms are, but about what brings this organization together and what is eating at its core.

There has been a lot of popular literature written about the one-minute manager, and managing by walking around and the authors of this book subscribe to this approach. It is amazing what you can learn in the first days while people are still trying to put their best foot forward and impart their words of wisdom to you, the newcomer.

Let us not go as far as the Godfather theory that the one who approaches you first is the traitor. Yet, we've found from our past experiences that the people who are very eager to reach and 'connect' with you during these first few hours or days are the ones you need to keep an eye on, though, of course, there are exceptions to every rule.

There are a few tricks of the trade that can help you understand and get the lay of the land in the fastest possible time. We suggest a few below:

As discussed in the 'Expanding the Circle' chapter,

Hold meetings as often as you can —formal and informal; be approachable, listen, and then mentally (or electronically) file away the comments, notes, and impressions you gather. This will always be a valuable source of information throughout your journey.

Read as much as you can. You will be surprised about the insights you can get from spending some time on the company's intranet or public email folder—see previous announcements, hires and fires, and pick up the tone of the place: is it formal, family oriented, a revolving door company, or a company that simply does not communicate its important issues?

Observe. Nobody said you have to lead meetings from day one. Watch out for body language, for power-hungry team members or peers, and start customizing your approach accordingly Once these informal approaches are running, you need to start your diagnostic of the current situation. It is important to note that the diagnostic phase is not to be rushed, as much as we would like to think that we 'got it', that we know what ails this company, and that we are ready to jump to the blueprint phase. Slow down, take your time and give this key phase its due course. In the appendix chapters, we include some of these tools:

Interviews: This is a formal interview process, where you take key stakeholders out of their every day work and chat for 1-2 hours. Have an agenda and a list of questions ready, but don't run it too rigidly; Allow for as much free thinking as prudent without losing track of what you need to uncover and discuss. Ask the questions you want to ask directly and without sugar coating; do not be rude, but do not be bashful. These interviews are practically the starting point for the process which you need to get the organization through in order to start by self-examining its ills and to get it on the road to recovery.

Surveys and Questionnaires. Yawn, you think; Well, think again. Looking back at all the experience we've had, we are still confident that what you can gather in anonymous and digital surveys and questionnaires is invaluable; It lets people express themselves and then lets you capture the thoughts, diagnoses, and remedies they suggest. Categorize, prioritize and adapt these suggestions and findings wherever possible. You may also be lucky enough to benefit from the results of surveys already done, but neatly stashed on someone's shelf.

Town hall meetings. Yawn again. Well, wrong again. Use these meetings to showcase your program (what you can share about it) and to get your sponsor in the limelight (more on that later).

Audit Reports. These are mentioned in chapter 12, for the purpose of identifying quick wins...Already, in the context of understanding the lay of the land and completing the corporate diagnostic process, they are invaluable. Review all internal and external reports (over the past 1 to 2 years). If anything, these reports will holistically reflect the corporate governance processes and performance, identify (and corroborate) the major process, technology, and people issues, and assign their respective priorities from a risk perspective.

It's important to keep in mind that this information-gathering exercise is not meant to get superficial insights nor is it for casual observation. You need to dig deep, question, explore, and catalogue what you've found out and uncovered.

You also need to keep in mind that even the most distant stakeholders are likely to cross-check what you've asked them and what information you sought and were given. Attempting mind games and intentional misinformation (power tripping) is a dangerous game that you do not want and cannot afford to play. In addition, you are not passing judgment on what you hear; your goal at this stage is to know as much as you can so you can pave the path toward moving forward.

Once the data collection process finishes, consolidate, analyze, verify and quantify! It is important to perform some due diligence to validate this raw diagnostic information, which will have a large impact on the blueprint structure and content. Aside from power trips and misinformation, humans have a tendency to process their information through many subconscious filters, like emotions, personal likes and dislikes, ambitions, hearsay, exaggeration, ego and the like. It is important to assess whether problems reported as high or low priority do really cause the purported dysfunction, or if they are merely a small blip on the corporate radar screen. This verification process is done through a variety of approaches and brainstorming sessions with tools such as affinity diagrams, cause and effect analysis, the Pareto principle (80/20 rule), prioritization scoring, and finally yet importantly, a SWOT analysis to round out the diagnostic.

Diagnostic studies can metamorphose into full-blown projects, with creeping project scopes and overly detailed analysis. Therefore, strict deadlines and assumptions (do's and don'ts) must be set from the start to control this task. For example, this diagnostic should not turn into a full-blown audit. You need to attempt to process various tasks in parallel so that by the end of the 3rd or 4th week all results are in. A rule of thumb is that you should not spend more than 4 to 6 weeks on this entire process.

With this reservoir of information and insights, you are ready to start preparing for your blueprint.

Summary: Preparing a complete diagnostic study very quickly is an important prerequisite for structuring and supporting your blueprint. The CxO can use unstructured approaches like the review of publicly available resources (intranet, public folders, etc.), in addition to a set of structured tools such as interviews, surveys, audit reports, and formal meetings. Document and verify the results using common frameworks and tools. Make sure this task does not get out of hand by ensuring awareness of its scope, approach and duration.

⌘   ⌘   ⌘

5. The Unpolished Diamonds

One of the great joys of being a newly hired Change Agent is to identify and bring into being a cadre of new stars from the ranks of the organization. An even greater joy is when these stars are staff members and leaders who were overlooked or discounted in the past by previous regimes or unfavorable circumstances.

As CxOs, we quickly come to the realization that we cannot effect all the necessary change alone, nor can we accomplish our mission(s) by hiring small armies of newcomers or worse, consultants and contractors. An effective change team needs a healthy mix of existing staff members who provide the organizational insights and knowledge as well as the new hires with new ideas and a zeal for change.

One of your early tasks should be to scan the troops for the unpolished diamonds, and bring them into the fold and spirit of change. This requires a sharp eye and good scouting skills.

My main job was developing talent. I was a gardener providing water and other nourishment to our top 750 people. Of course, I had to pull out some weeds, too.

Jack Welch

Look for second-tier managers with a reputation for being effective but are constrained by the inadequacies of their reporting managers. These leaders will jump at the opportunity to prove their worth and showcase their abilities and skills. This should be your first option.

Another source are young, well-educated staff members who are informally involved with cross-functional work and would love the opportunity to expand their horizons, work with multiple groups, and lead change efforts. They see these change programs as a means to another step up the corporate ladder.

Look also for superstars that did not live up to the organization's expectations or worse, their own. Dig deep into the reasons—is it lack of training, lack of leadership, or simply not being in the right place at the right time? They will be eager to dust off their images of unmet expectations to silence the doubters. In the past, we have had great success with previously sidelined employees who are now on a winning team.

Another group is the casualties of previously aborted initiatives and programs. They will be harder to win over because they were burnt before and have heard all the rhetoric. However, if you can win them over, they will be a great asset to your programs; they will arrive with invaluable lessons-learned and insights on what works and what does not in this organization. Once committed, beware—these individuals become pit bulls that will not let go until they deliver results.

Other places to look in are staff members who've been assigned to special projects that are going nowhere or have recently-completed projects and people returning from ex-pat assignments who are eager to re-establish their connections in the organization.

Once you bring these unpolished diamonds on board, it is imperative to customize an approach to hone their skills and close any delivery gaps they might have. This requires constant interaction and communication. There is a confidence level for you to rebuild and an image to restore. As they gain more confidence and become more engaged, just let go of the reins and give them all the room they need to grow and deliver. You will be amazed by the energy they will have and the desire to succeed they will exhibit. If you are lucky enough to identify and recruit a handful of these talents, they will do the job of a small army of consultants and be your strongest allies. Not to mention they will be the walking advertisement to the rest of the organization that you mean business and that you are committed to a genuine change program that builds on the organization's strengths and soldiers, rather than a 'down your throat' approach that never works.

As your team is growing and the energy is building, you need to be aware of the backlash that this might create. The same managers who failed to harness the energy and drive of these unpolished diamonds will feel the pressure; they will have to answer the question about why this person didn't thrive and succeed on their team, but is now a star on your team. Prepare yourself for cheap shots and covert resistance. As long as you are ready for it, you will be able to handle and deflect it; this will only make you more valuable and credible in the eyes of your newly founded team.

Sadly, a common side effect is that once these people show their true colors and are working at a higher level of delivery, they are to be poached. This is natural, and you will need to make some tough decisions and let go of some of these star players if it is in their best interest and the interest of the organization. But rest assured that the goodwill you've created in identifying them as potential stars and helping them achieve their potential will never fade or be forgotten. We still get calls from these unpolished diamonds from two or three organizations back, in a way we've turned into their mentors and sponsors, and nothing gives us more professional joy than to see them grow and prosper.

An example of where to look for hidden talent comes from a past experience we had while working with a financial institution in a southern state within the first few days of project start-up. It became apparent to us that one of the line managers was an exceptional leader and possessed excellent delivery skills. However, her director kept complaining about her skills and tried several times to get her off the project. When we dug deeper into the matter, we found out that she joined his group as part of a husband and wife team that was relocated from another regional office. Her husband was heavily recruited and she was hired after he joined. The director could not get over the fact that she was 'forced' on his group and could not see past that to recognize her skills. He readily endorsed our recommendation that she be transferred to another group that was being formed, and our star employee went on to a more accommodating and supportive group where she continued to deliver superior results. It was the shortsightedness of her first director that cost a couple of years being labeled as an under-performer, and all it took was a transfer where she could shine and deliver. Look for these hidden treasures; they are all over the organization.

Lastly, prepare yourself for some disappointment, as some of these unpolished diamonds will turn out to be under-achievers. The best scouting and the best supportive environment will not make them stars. This is an unpleasant fact, and rather than becoming bitter about it, you should feel good that you have taken a chance on someone even if they have failed to capitalize on it. In these cases, gently ease them off the team (others will be very supportive) and maintain the course. It is not a failing of the approach; some people have limitations that require prohibitively lengthy coaching efforts to raise them to the required level or are simply duds.

Now that we have looked at the internal resource landscape, let us view the other dimension of the HR world. There are other sources of great talent out there, whether you are working with competitors or consultants, and there is no avoiding it; you will need external recruits. The most difficult part comes in the balancing act between luring, recruiting and maintaining these resources and on the other hand managing the morale of your current staff, who will quickly notice the arrival of new highly-paid talent and start wondering what is in store for them. Moreover, believe us, no number of soothing emails or counseling will extinguish this fire. The best approach to manage this common situation is:

- Be frank with your employees. Share the reasons for why you need to bring in new talent, and why it usually costs more to entice talented people to move to a new firm.
- Create a project bonus pool, and distribute to all employees on the project in a manner commensurate with their performance and participation, and conditional on remaining on board until sometime after the completion of your project.
- Discuss with the HR department the available options to advance talented employees and reward them for their achievements through various reward programs.
- Prepare a skills-gap analysis and suitable training programs to show current employees that the company is serious about investing in them.

Summary: Look for hidden talents and unpolished diamonds in the organization; Build them up and sustain their energy; they will be your greatest asset. Let them go if you have to, and cut your losses when they do not work out.

⌘ ⌘ ⌘

6. The Blueprint

With the right pieces in place and an initial assessment done, as CxOs we now need to progress to the first practical stage of effecting the changes. To accomplish that, a blueprint or manifesto of changes needs to be developed. Developing this blueprint requires careful timing; if completed too early, then some of the findings and actions will be viewed as premature and baseless; if delayed too long, then the value of the findings and the urgency of remedies will start to diminish, and the perception of the CxO's effectiveness will be brought under a spotlight. The timing will vary greatly from one organization to another, but there are few tips that can help you judge when the time is right to draw this blueprint:

- When the initial rounds of meetings and interviews are completed; when you are comfortable in identifying trends and similarities in the issues raised and needs for change.
- When you start developing a clearer path towards improving the current situation that can be translated into coherent and persuasive arguments.
- When your team is in place and the organization (peers, team members, and powers-that-be) start expressing their desire to see the next stage.

Background consultations are crucial as you put together your blueprint. It's very important that the model used fits in the fabric of the organization; some are very well-suited to a military style set of orders that are adhered to and followed with precision, while some cultures will require a more consultative (yet firm) approach to build the right level of consensus and buy-in. It is critical to customize your approach to the environment you are working in—even if you favor a style based on previous successes.

A typical blueprint will include key components such as:

- A holistic initial assessment of the areas needing change or improvement; this should be an objective assessment based on facts and findings that can be substantiated if and when challenged (and they will be).
- The source from which the approach and methodology were derived. Was it from meetings, auditors' and inspectors' reports, previous project findings, Sponsor directives, walk-arounds, etc.? A good approach mixes all of the above and separates facts from assumptions and emotions.
- The blueprint then should outline the ambitions of the change program, the destination or journey as the case may be, and why these ambitions are appropriate, and then deftly and tactfully tie the findings and approach with the goals. Be creative and strive for a tight alignment with the corporate strategy and ambitions.
- Milestones—how soon will changes start occurring? What lags and what follows? How to sequence the changes in a way to achieve the most results quickly, without exposing the organization to additional risks? This is very important in cases where HR or people-related changes are the cornerstone of the change program. It is important to note here that quick-win goals

require a thorough analysis to ensure their feasibility and real impact. Unachievable or useless quick-wins at the start of the program can be very damaging to the credibility of the entire approach.

- The core and extended teams who will carry out these changes and how they will do it. Again, make sure that the blueprint and approach are customized for your organization's culture and tolerance for change.

A good blueprint should be both <u>realistic and aggressive</u>; it should reflect the realities of the organization, its culture and discomfort threshold, while charting a course that aggressively moves it forward toward its desired destination. Do not be too shy to dream a bit, and show your aggressive side in creating this blueprint; this is one of the reasons you were mandated with this task in the first place.

Any good blueprint will require a conscious sales effort (more on that in the Debut Presentation Chapter), but even in drafting and outlining the changes, try to stay away from the academic and dry approach, and make it a live document that your audience (core and expanded) can relate to and rally behind. Sell it!

A technique that works very well in putting together effective blueprints is to highlight the changes that have already been accomplished in the time since the CxO joined. These might be small or even minor improvements, but they will create a powerful perception of change and will aid in building credibility for the change program, as they demonstrate that changes are already underway and not just plans in fancy presentations.

Referring to previous change programs or attempts is a double-edged sword. On the one hand, when it's time to present your blueprint, the comparison to previous attempts is inevitable. By acknowledging prior initiatives, you show that you have done your homework and learned from previous mistakes. On the other hand, you need to be careful not to taint your work with previous failures or to lose the support of prior sponsors/owners. A successful technique is to involve the latter as consultants to the new change program, thus demonstrating that we have listened, learnt our lessons and obtained unanimous buy-in.

At this point, there are two schools of thought on the initial syndication of the blueprint. Both work. The first is to get the change program sponsor (usually the Sponsor) to approve the blueprint and then communicate it to the rest of the organization as a fait accompli. The other is to keep the blueprint in draft mode until after the initial or debut presentation, and then seal the program. Again, both will work, and will depend on the culture and the ability of the sponsor to drive change through the organization. Regardless of the approach taken, by continually involving peers and stakeholders in the drafting of the blueprint, you will be able to mitigate potential resistance.

The blueprint is a live document and not frozen in time; this means that it should be reviewed and presented repeatedly depending on the extent of modifications. The findings are subject to change, and timelines can be revisited. Thinking of the blueprint as a snapshot of a time in the life of the organization is a sure way to doom the whole change program. Findings and priorities can change at any given time. The entire change program needs to be flexible, modular and relevant. As the change agent and leader of this effort, you need to remain vigilant and aware of the relevance of the program and its individual components throughout its course.

⌘　⌘　⌘

7. The Debut Presentation

Armed with your blueprint, and ideally a consensus and acceptance, it is now *Showtime*!

Not to heap more pressure on the CxOs, but this debut presentation—when the blueprint and change roadmap make their formal appearance—is, to borrow an old expression, a "make-it or break-it" step.

Got your attention? Good. Preparing for this debut presentation is important, despite the prep work has gone into designing the blueprint, and the enthusiasm and kudos you got from your peers or even the Sponsor on your brilliant ideas for change. This presentation sets the tone and lays the tracks for accomplishing your change program and carrying out your mandate.

An important and elementary question that you need to be able to answer is, "what do you want to accomplish in this presentation?" Many a debut presentation has gone horribly wrong because the presenter focused on the following:

- How quickly he or she has been able to understand the problems of the organization and how sharp his/her eye for identifying the solutions. Yes, you need to communicate this (remember, you *are* selling), but do not do it at the expense of the value the change program will provide the organization.
- How well versed and familiar the presenter is with the latest in improvement techniques, tools, industry best practices and methodologies, and how this wealth of knowledge will be deployed to make it happen.

Important, yes, but too much focus on the mechanics and too strong a desire to impress with form rather than substance will turn the audience off.

- How <u>bad the situation is</u>. This can take several forms: that the company's problems are so bad yet so obvious and that the presenter is aghast that things have deteriorated to such a state. Another form is to demean all previous attempts at improving the organization, and showboat on how *this* initiative and program will be so different, staffed with the right people, and endowed with the tools to get the job done. Both messages will turn the audience against the presenter and the program, since we all know deep down what the problems are, and have a desire to see improvements, but how many of us like to have this message rubbed in our faces?

On the other hand, many presentations fell flat because the presenter did not perform any of the following tasks in advance:

- <u>Anticipate negative questions from the "darkside".</u> In practically most companies, one or more of the senior members attending the presentation will be hostile to the change program or CxO (by association with the recruiting party i.e. Sponsor, simply because change is not in his/her interest). S/he will demonstrate this during the presentation through barbed questions, Byzantine arguments, or trapdoor discussions. It is good practice to play the devil's advocate in advance of the presentation by anticipating attacks on the blueprint/program.

This can be done in many ways. One would be to ask the collaborative members of management about the historical causes for the darkside's opposition to the change program. Secondly, you can ask the "darkside" themselves, in good faith, and assuring them that their concerns will be addressed in the program. However, keep your guard up during the presentation!

- Diligently anticipate potential questions on all angles of every initiative outlined in the blueprint. Remember, this is your first presentation and you cannot be over-prepared. Ask yourself the five W's (and one H!) on every project attribute within the overall program. Attributes could be the scope, cost, approach, project manager, beneficiaries, duration, assumptions, etc. Use tools such as mind-maps, Pareto charts, affinity diagrams and the like to ensure that the program/project addresses root causes and will provide the planned benefits. Brainstorm with your team on how to tackle any potential negative or "smart-alecky" questions that might be thrown around, whether in good faith or for show value in front of the powers that be.

Another good tip is to present the material informally and on a personal basis with all the key attendees; this is an old consultant's trick, such that by the time the audience enters the room, most have seen the crucial parts of the presentation and have had a chance to give their input. By giving them an opportunity in private to voice their opinions and provide you with guidance (adopt it if you can), they now come to feel allegiance to what will be presented and to the presenter and will support and cheer during the presentation, as they were given an insider's view of the changes to come and would have gained a sense of ownership and participation in the process.

> *"An example of debut presentations that didn't go well is a large European FMG company that retained consultants to review and recommend changes to its worldwide infrastructure. In numerous meetings with the CEO and CFO, the consultants were inundated with all that was wrong with the infrastructure group; these comments were duly captured and incorporated in the assessment and blueprint. But when the blueprint was presented, the presenter was viciously attacked for coming up with a shallow assessment of the facts and an improvement program that would never work. When debriefing after the meeting, the stunned and bruised consultant was told that, it was customary for the CEO and CFO to see these presentations beforehand and to give their input. Having been included merely in the general audience, they felt slighted and marginalized. Lesson learned."*

The mechanics of the presentation, such as the delivery mode (i.e. through Power Point, or as a sit down meeting to review hard copies), the time of day, the number of attendees and other logistical matters are agreed jointly with the Sponsor. A good rule of thumb is to keep it short, simple and positive.

Another area of debate is who should present the blueprint. Is it the designated CxO, the sponsor, or the entire change team? While there are no hard and fast rules, we found it most useful and effective for the Sponsor to open and close the session, and the CxO to present the body of the blueprint. Getting the change team members in front of this audience can backfire; remember some of these team members might still be associated with previous failures or have been reassigned from their prior functions. The CxO should assert his/her authority on the entire change program and employ the presence and backgrounds of the change team to aid in the presentation, but own up to the blueprint and the change mandate.

The wrap up of the debut presentation needs to be managed skillfully. Your goal should be to close on a positive yet serious note. Your mandate is for change, and change is never easy, but the outcome can be positive when the change is for the right reasons and in the right way.

Assure your audience that you will keep providing them with frequent updates and presentations with a focus on progress, risks and achievements.

Summary: A good debut presentation delivers the message of change and builds the grassroots support for the initiative by highlighting the need for change and the benefits for all without singling out people or functions and without using the presentation as a vehicle to demonstrate the presenter's skills and prowess. Keep it focused and positive and end it on a high note.

⌘　⌘　⌘

8. Rules of the Game

With your expanded circle in place and knowledge of the organization, its culture and insights gained and catalogued, you now need to turn your attention to the rules of the game.

These rules are for you veteran CxOs out there as well as newbie executives. They apply to the change effort and change team as well as to the organization as a whole as it interacts with the change program and team. Throughout the book we have promoted and advised taking a softer more collaborative approach to designing and implementing the change manifesto. This is the one and only time where we advocate a more formal and firm course of action. We'll explain why as we go through this chapter.

Rule#1: Set and implement communication protocols. How will the change team communicate internally and externally; what is written down and what is verbal? Where will this information and written exchanges be stored and how? What response times are set for answering queries and how to close and track outstanding issues? What are the project reporting standards, reporting lines, and issue escalation points?

Rule#2: The scope of the blueprint is not up for debate. Secure agreement and endorsement, and stick with it. For tips and best practices on how to manage with expanding scope and demands, please refer to the "Momentum" chapter.

Rule#3: The buck stops here. Clearly identify and enforce the choice of a final arbitrator and arbitration mechanism for thorny issues. If the stakeholders agree on a change task—among themselves or with the team—who will arbitrate and how? The final decision should rest with you (with proper endorsement from the sponsor). Do not let a power or decision vacuum fester, or you will jeopardize your entire change blueprint.

Rule#4: Timelines are sacred. Do not under any circumstances let timelines slip (as much as humanly possible). This is a test of your blueprint's viability and your ability to execute on time and to deliver results. We cannot stress this issue enough.

Rule#5: People will complain. You are neither their parent nor their best friend. Listen and empathize, but do not waver. It is amazing how childish and petty some of the most senior team members will be, and how they will whine. Let them vent—within reason—but cut it off, and do not change your scope or timeline. Organizations will ALWAYS be understaffed, will ALWAYS be too busy, and will ALWAYS be missing key skills and resources. These are facts of life. However, a change blueprint is also a fact of life. Deal with it. For the perpetual whiners, recommend temporary options for their project teams, such as working overtime, on weekends, outsourcing nonessential tasks, helping them (lobby the Sponsor), offloading non-critical projects to free up more resources, allocating rewards for meeting deadlines, etc.

Rule#6: There is a reason why they call them best practices. Do not doubt yourself and your tools; Stay the course and the results will follow. As we discuss in a later chapter, you should be cognizant of the "this is how we used to do it" trap but at the same time, drawing on best practices is a rule you cannot do without.

Rule#7: Resources, logistics and motivation. All employee movements, handovers of responsibilities, availability (during and outside working hours) and work allocation are to be choreographed and planned in advance among project stakeholders in line with the blueprint schedule. It is also a common issue that an ad-hoc employee vacation, reallocation of SME's to different units, lack of proper handovers and training and over-allocation of work by stakeholders may reduce the effectiveness of the project resource pool considerably. It is equally important to agree on employee overtime standards to set up expectations among teams on the occasional need to work outside normal working hours and on motivational rewards (i.e. end-of-project bonus) to mitigate the risk of employee (mainly SME) turnover during the project.

Rule#8: Roles, responsibilities and accountability. Clearly state ownership and accountability, as they are critical. Set these guidelines and procedure from day one and breakdown to the stakeholder level. This outlines accountability and remedial actions in case of delays.

Rule#9: Stay out of the limelight. If you refer back to our opening chapter on the relationship between the designated CxO and his/her sponsors, and as we go through the progression of the change program, at this point in the process, you need to be cognizant of, and on the lookout for, a monster that's likely to rear its ugly head. We are talking about stepping in the limelight of your sponsor!

In an ideal corporate world, your sponsor would be your biggest ally and supporter. He/she would applaud your achievements and carry the torch of success forward, and as your successes roll in he/she would be at the sidelines cheering you on and asking for more. This doesn't always happen in the real world!

Before we delve into this unsavory topic, please note that our views should not be misconstrued or taken as blatant criticism of sponsors (hey, we have to work too). Nevertheless, it is a painful reality that you CxOs, consultants, or newly hired executives need to consider as you tackle your change blueprints and manage this tenuous and fragile relationship.

Even the most secure, accomplished and confident sponsor is not immune to these bouts of jealousy and resistance as your blueprint is progressing and the organization's issues and ailments are exposed. This is normal. At the end of the day, all of these issues and problems happened and accumulated on their watch. Give them credit for recognizing the need for change and for engaging a brilliant CxO like you. Also, recognize the frailties of the human ego.

Except in those cases when the CxO's mandate and blueprint are launched at the same time a sponsor or new sponsor joins an organization as part of a new regime (usually after an acquisition or major problems), these frictions and conflicts are more likely to happen than not.

To get a better idea of the issues you might face, examine the following symptoms closely and see if you can relate to them:

1. Is your Sponsor asking you to scale back the scope and reach of the blueprint after you have successfully delivered the first 1-2 wins?
2. Is your Sponsor giving you the talk about not ruffling feathers and managing your peers' and employees' feelings and insecurities as you are rolling through your change blueprint?
3. Is your Sponsor conspicuously missing in action from status meetings, conflict resolution meetings and launch and wrap-up meetings?

4. Are quasi- or pseudo- Sponsors emerging with the blessing of your Sponsor and chipping away at your change blueprint?

5. Are you getting the silent treatment, the communication vacuum or worse—are you left to fend for yourself and your change program without any support from your Sponsor?

If any of the above is occurring, then dear reader, you have stepped in the limelight of your sponsor. We often wonder why accomplished and high caliber sponsors react in this manner, but as CxOs, we should not really be surprised. They are human after all.

If this happens—and chances are you may find yourself in this situation—do not lose heart. We recommend the following courses of action, in addition to the usual every-day change activities:

A. <u>Try to have a soft heart-to-heart with your sponsor.</u> Do not criticize; do not come across as wounded or a victim; focus on the value his/her support lends to the change blueprint and how the recent seeming waning of that support is starting to affect the progress and the success of the change blueprint. This is not personal, and it should never be a "you promised; you told me; you asked me" affair. Stay focused on the issue of the overall value of the change process and the sponsor's support of it, and how the success of the change blueprint will be a good reflection and a win for the entire organization and the sponsor primarily.

B. <u>Consider scaling back</u> some of your blueprint activities and/or the pace of change, as long as it does not affect the integrity and credibility of the overall blueprint. A bit of fine-tuning and picking the right battles to fight might be the best way to assuage the negative feelings.

C. <u>Never ever criticize or assign blame for the mistakes of the past or the problems of the organization to the sponsor</u>, publicly or privately. You will be surrounded by squadrons of people who love nothing more than to report to the Sponsor your negative views of their personalities, management styles, or shortcomings. The most well intended comment will come back to haunt you. And keep in mind that even if you are not getting any "face time" with your sponsor, their antennae are always up and they are constantly watching and monitoring your progress and actions.

D. <u>Channel some of the credit and attention to your sponsor</u>, whether deserved or not, but be subtle and tactful, do not "kiss up", but also do not rub their noses in previous failures.

E. Take your sales, communication and change skills to a higher level. <u>Practice what you preach</u>.

F. If these approaches fail, <u>start planning your exit</u>!

In the face of such internal resistance and wasted energy, do not lose heart, and do not get discouraged. Expect this and plan for it... Stay focused and go back to the basics. This is human nature; logic will not always prevail.

In brief: Foster a healthy relationship with your sponsor, but expect resistance and possibly jealousy. The more you plan and anticipate this, the better you will be able to deal with it, and turn it to the benefit of your team and blueprint.

Rule #10: Manage the Quasi-Sponsors

A lot of literature is available on the different personalities at work from the bullies, the snipers, the naysayers, and other colorful characters that we have the pleasure of working side by side with in our careers and throughout our change programs and blueprint processes.

Another type that can be poisonous and detrimental to your mandate as the new hero of change is the senior executive we like to call "Quasi-Sponsor". Let us elaborate.

In many organizations, there are usually power circles within which most of the senior executives orbit. One or two senior executives, who in their own minds have an unalienable right to be running the organization and see the Sponsor as a usurper, dominate these circles. You do not have to look very hard to identify these peacocks. Look in the ranks of long-serving Senior VPs, CxOs, and rising stars in the business development units.

As you embark on implementing your change blueprint, it is crucial and vital that you identify these power bases and "Quasi-Sponsors" early on and devise a strategy to get them on your side or at least to neutralize their effect. It would not be an exaggeration to say that a good part of the reason why your change blueprint is important is because these executives have been building and fortifying their power bases at the expense of the Sponsor's effectiveness and the welfare of the organization.

Before we start devising strategies for dealing with these senior executives, it's important to understand why the organization has allowed this fragmented power base to develop and persist, as this background will shape the strategy. These power bases and quasi-Sponsors emerge due to cultural fractures:

- Has the company gone through a recent merger or acquisition, which resulted in a crowded executive structure? Are some of the affected executives previous Sponsors or Sponsors-in-waiting?
- Are some of these Quasi-Sponsors board or political appointees? This is more common than we think. These can be a very dangerous specimen of executives to deal with as they feel they are above the rules of the game.

Regardless of the motivation, circumstances or background, when you are designing and embarking on implementing your change blueprint, the following can be helpful in reducing the risk of sniping, sabotage or resistance from these power bases:

- <u>Rule#1: Do not try to play them off against each other</u>. It will never work, and you will be caught in the crossfire. As a newcomer to the organization and a leader of change, do not fall into the trap of underestimating the shared history these people have and the intricate deals that were struck and will be struck to protect their positions and keep the dance going.
- <u>Rule#2: Do not count on Sponsor support.</u> Even the most macro, detached Sponsor is aware of what is going on in the organization. They might have their own agendas and power plays. Going to the Sponsor for support (above the norm) will only make things worse, as he or she might take it as criticism of their leadership style. After all, as we have noted, this is all happening on their watch.
- <u>Rule#3: Do not try to fix this problem</u>. Your mandate is a change mandate, and if you have done your

homework and got the right approvals and endorsements, this is more than plenty to keep you busy and focused. What we experience as CxOs is a daily deluge of complaints and requests for change from the troops who are suffering from these Quasi-Sponsors. While we're not advocating ignoring or turning a blind eye to these problems, unless it is a prerequisite to implement your change blueprint, steer clear of these power struggles, and let them fight their own fights.

- Rule #4: As we discussed in the blueprint and debut presentation chapters, get everyone involved, and the Quasi-Sponsors are no exception. However, you must be cognizant of their motivations and be prepared to decline some of their input if you truly believe that it stems from ulterior motives and will not improve—or worse—will harm the change blueprint. This is easier said than done, but this might mean the difference between a credible and successful change blueprint and a watered-down, politicized blueprint that is written off as a tool to serve a certain group or leader.

Another common but dangerous practice that we have encountered is the "fighting by proxy" approach. This is where the Sponsor or other leaders manipulate and use the change program or other leaders in the organization to fight their fights. We have experienced this first-hand when working with an organization where the Sponsor wanted to be everyone's friend, so the CxOs let the consultants fight his fights. Worse, he nominated two of his senior executives as the designated hatchet men who went around the organization executing his wishes and demands. It was no surprise to quickly identify both as

Quasi-Sponsors who single-handedly caused most of the problems that required a change blueprint in the first place.

In brief: Understanding the culture of the organization goes beyond getting familiar with the mission statements and annual report; it also goes beyond casual meetings and encounters with the staff at large. Understating the power bases and power plays is important for all CxOs as it can greatly affect their chances of success. However, be careful not to be dragged in these power plays and become a pawn.

Rule#11: Expect broken promises

Few things can be more disappointing and downright demoralizing than when faced with the first broken promise after joining a new organization.

The higher the level we join at and the wider our mandate, the worse the feeling we get when we discover that some of the promises that lured us to this new job and new organization have not, or will not, be kept.

Unusual, rare, unlikely? We think not. If you joined an organization in the past or are contemplating joining one, prepare yourself for this unpleasant experience, and most importantly, learn how to deal with it, and even come out ahead.

The promises we are talking about are not the financial ones or other benefits, i.e. how many vacation days you get, or which club membership the company will cover. It is safe to assume that enough time was given to negotiating these details and that we work for moral and honest organizations. The broken promises we refer to here are the ones that go to the heart of our ability to carry out our mission and mandates which, in severe cases, can render us completely ineffective.

The following are a few examples of such broken promises and the motives behind them, and most importantly, a suggested mechanism to deal with them.

Now that you are on the job, and if you have followed some of the advice we have been giving in this book, hopefully you have started to feel your way around the organization and built a strong team of allies; your plan of action is drawn up and communicated, and the results are starting to show. Then the first surprise appears:

- Your mandate for change included direct responsibility for several functions which are interrelated, and an effective change program will require you having the authority to directly influence these functions. Yet a few weeks into the job, <u>some of your functions are reassigned to another executive</u>, or worse, to the Sponsor, and you are given a feeble explanation after the fact. Example: a senior engineer was tasked with overhauling the Premises and Facilities function of an organization, and the mandate included direct responsibility for the Procurement function as its part of managing the Premises and Facilities and at the outset is one of the keys to turning the group around. A few weeks into the job, by way of an interoffice memo, the Procurement function was re-assigned to the CFO. The motive force behind this was intense lobbying carried out by the CFO (who was under pressure to show cost savings) to assume responsibility for this function which promised to yield substantial savings, at the expense of the change program planned by the new Head of Premises and Facilities. Faced with this abrupt change, our friend stormed into the CEO's office asking for an explanation and was placated with a few soothing words, as the Sponsor had decided (for whatever reasons he had) to yield to the CFO. Flash for-ward: the newly ap-pointed Head of Premises and Facilities redrafted his change program and expected results to show a less optimistic picture of improvements that could be achieved due to the breakdown in reporting which re-sulted in renewed dia-logue with the CEO

Synergies are something that the CEO basically has to force to happen, because organi-zations are, generally, like bodies in motion that tend to stay in motion. It's very hard to get big organizations to change. And it takes really a very powerful mandate to force things to happen.

John Malone

and CFO and joint reporting of Procurement. Ideal scenario? No, but a pragmatic one. By highlighting the results of this broken promise, the CxO was able to salvage his change program and work within the im-perfections of the organization.

- Your original mandate included a team of senior lead-ers pulled from their current positions to form a spe-cial task force and carry out the change mandate. You take the time to interview these leaders, and build your change program and customize it based on their backgrounds and abilities. But to your dismay, <u>less than 50% of these leaders join your team;</u> the rest are either retained by their current groups or assigned to the new golden boy and the Sponsor's new pet project (look at the Musical Pedestals concept in the next rule for more details). Faced with this disturbing develop-ment, our Change Agent can either scrap or curtail the change program, which is a lose-lose scenario. Another approach that might work is to reach out to the leaders who did not join and find out if they truly wanted to be on board, and if they did, making them part of the change program on an advisory basis. This flattering compromise should appease their reporting managers and assist the change agent in securing their assistance. In some cases, these 'consulting team members' will build their own case and extricate themselves to work full time on the change program.

These examples can easily stretch to include <u>reduced budgets</u>, <u>reduced advertising</u>, <u>delayed timeframes</u>, <u>new locations</u> and a slew of other broken promises. We will come face to face with these broken promises.

As CxOs, it behooves us to practice what we preach and try to make the best of the situation, and at the same time, be honest with our organizations and ourselves. If the cuts are too deep, and changes are such that our mandates and our change programs cannot survive, then we need to prepare ourselves to make some tough choices.

In brief: Prepare yourself to live without some of the tools promised, examine the situation and motives and try to come up with creative ways to lessen their negative impact. Be the true CxO that you are.

<u>Rule #12: Avoid Scope Creep, and the 'Musical Pedestal'</u>

Some Sponsors have a rather annoying habit of simply believing in the new guy to an unrealistic degree. However, how can this be a problem? Let us explain the concept of the "musical pedestal":

Upon joining the organization as the savior and miracle worker who will fix everything in no time, change the face of the organization and weed out trouble, your Sponsor confers on you the status of "Golden Boy/Girl"; you are the one to whom he listens in meetings, the one he agrees with regardless of how unconvincing you sound; More seriously, you are the one he tells your peers to be more/less like, "I wish you all could be as open and forthcoming in our weekly sessions as Bob here", and the fatal move that Sponsors love to make, which is to start piling responsibilities on you that they feel your peers have not been able to deliver on up to his/her expectations.

Why is this bad, you say? Let us examine it closely:

First, you are likely to have entered the organization with a higher title and/or higher compensation than the people sitting around the table with you. They had to pay a premium to get you in the first place, didn't they? In addition, you are now likely looking after areas or attempting to turn around functions some of them had before you, or worse, who were the "golden child" months or even weeks ago.

Secondly, you do not have the record of accomplishment in this company yet, nor do you have allies who can back you up, least of whom is the person at the head of the table, so you are already starting with a considerable handicap. In addition, if you start waxing wise and spouting about how you used to do it before at your old company, you might as well pack up and go home now.

Thirdly and most importantly, you need to be honest with yourself. Are these new responsibilities or initiatives truly within your capabilities? Alternatively, are you intoxicated by this aura of invincibility that the boss is giving you, while in reality, you will not fare any better than others have before you?

If we look ahead at the typical outcome of this scenario, some or all of the following will happen (we have seen it firsthand and experienced it as well). Your peers and partners will turn on you from the start. Rather than giving you genuine support, you will get lip service and in some cases blatant (or covert) sabotage as noted above.

Next, you will likely lose focus given all of the additional responsibilities (i.e. "handicaps"), which will happen at the expense of your original mandate which was ambitious to start with; You will find yourself fighting multiple battles with little or no support from the organization, all the while trying to shore up your knowledge in new areas that you are unfamiliar with and can't truly contribute to and trying very hard not to disappoint the boss.

Lastly, these unrealistic expectations from the boss and the natural slow pace of delivery of numerous initiatives and functions will start to irk your fearless leader, who now feels that he/she has been let down yet again, by another golden girl/boy. How we have wished at times that we could give some of these Sponsors a dose of reality so they could see the mistakes they keep making repeatedly.

At this point, you are likely to be confused, stressed, and quite threatened. You are not delivering on your original mandate, the boss is not as accessible as s/he used to be, your brilliant ideas and suggestions are being shot down in meetings and your peers are giving you the "I told you so" look.

Moreover, what is that you see? Another golden child has emerged? How can that be? *I am* the savior, *I am* the miracle worker. This cannot be happening to me.

Then the axe falls, the new golden boy/girl gets all the attention, and slowly some of your projects and mandates are reassigned to him/her. In addition, you are now a bystander as the pattern repeats itself.

The advice to all of you joining new organizations as the designated CxOs or saviors is to stick to your original mandates no matter how tempting it is to take on more work in your honeymoon period, and to make allies and friends as early as you can. Do not get seduced or intoxicated by your new-found status. As easily as it was given, it will be taken back.

Now this is easier said than done. How can you say 'No' to someone who truly believes in you and wants to be supportive, and how can you resist the temptation to show all these old timers who were asleep at the wheel what the new kid on the block can do? Difficult? Yes. Impossible? No.

Proceed carefully and remember, at the end of the day or year, we are all judged by what we delivered on our original orders; all the extra work and sexy-sounding projects and initiatives won't matter or count if the fundamentals of our jobs were not fulfilled.

Rule# 13: Stay clear of the Silver Bullet Trap

The Silver Bullet Syndrome afflicts managers and senior executives from all walks of corporate life, from different levels, industries and across multiple responsibilities. It is an addiction to the short cut.

Intrigued? Here is how it works:

Most of us as CxOs or senior executives know deep down in our hearts what ails our organizations and the problems that need to be tackled and fixed. We also realize how painful it is going to be to eradicate these problems for the last time—from a cost point of view, the cultural impact, people issues, etc. So when faced with the chronic problems, our natural instinct is to find a less painful course of action.

If you find yourself, your boss or even your subordinates thinking along these lines, then beware, you have the Silver Bullet Syndrome. Here are some examples:

1. "If we can only fix this one problem, the rest will take care of itself". Example, a retailer that suffers from a sub-standard level of service at its sales outlets that is costing lost sales and a shrinking customer base. To fix the problem effectively, the company needed to examine its product range, pricing, workflow at the outlets, the quality of the staff, etc. However, what did they do about it? They changed the signage and color scheme, to increase customer appeal. If we only make our outlets more inviting, our customer-related problems will disappear and the rest will take care of itself. Never works!

2. "If we can only hire this person, the rest of the organization will rally behind him/her and we can hit our numbers." Another classic silver bullet. Example, the senior leadership of an organization recognized that people issues are at the heart of their problems, which are exhibited in high turnover, union problems, employee theft, etc. Rather than examining its HR policies and making tough and financially costly changes, the company kept changing its HR directors at breakneck speed; Without any real empowerment or a sincere effort to implement new ideas, you can guess the results. Never works!

   > *The first rule of any technology used in a business is that automation applied to an efficient operation will magnify the efficiency. The second is that automation applied to an inefficient operation will magnify the inefficiency.*
   >
   > **Bill Gates**

3. "If we can only get this new system, the rest will take care of itself". Example, a large distributor which suffered from high

cost of sales, long collection periods, bad customer debts and excessively high returns (most of which were caused by a poor procurement policy, wrong product mix and an inefficient geographic distribution) proceeded to spend millions on a new system that basically mirrored the existing mess and spat out the same problems, rather than tackling the heart of the trouble. Never works!

An example of the addiction to silver bullets and their magical powers is an investment firm we worked with and was a rare case where we had to pull out. This particular company was managed by a driven and ambitious individual who unfortunately knew little about the business but got to where he was by a combination of charisma, being in the right place in the right time and a healthy dose of luck. To mask this lack of knowledge, the company suffered greatly from an addiction to silver bullets. One month it was a newly- hired executive, who was billed as the savior, then it was a cost reduction program, then an expansion program, then a product innovation program, then it was consultants, then technology and the list goes on and on. Each one of these initiatives could have yielded positive and meaningful results had they been initiated for the right reasons and given enough time and attention to deliver results, but taken as quick fixes without proper planning and focus, they ended up aborted attempts at effecting change. As hard as we tried we just could not break the cycle and get through to the Sponsor the need for a holistic approach to change and a concerted and well choreographed sequence of events.

4. "If we can only engage these consultants, the rest will take care of itself." Our favorite silver bullet. Usually you hear these from senior executives or Sponsors who

pride themselves on having great vision and brilliant ideas, and who blame the problems of the organization on the inability to implement and translate their great vision into reality. So rather than engage their troops, and be willing to accept changes/criticism of their ideas, they pull in teams and teams of consultants who basically regurgitate the same half-baked ideas in fancier terms, with unrealistic plans that nobody buys and nobody commits to implement. While the initiating executive gets a fleeting sense of validation, s/he invariably finds himself and the organization with the same issues, but with more consultant plans and ideas that they failed to implement yet again. Never works!

5. "This year is practically over; we'll take care of it next year". Example, an organization that is habitually under-performing and consistently does not meet its budget, due to a poor budgeting process, lack of strategy, poor internal communication and lack of leadership. The silver bullet; let us use the remainder of this year to fix our problems, and be ready to hit the ground running by January 2nd. The scary part is that this is a direct quote from a senior management meeting held in April in a Jan-Dec financial calendar year. Rather than rolling up their sleeves, truly tackling the problem and salvaging 8 to 9 months of the current year, the decision is (and it happened for five consecutive years) to write off the year patch problems and be ready next year. Never works!

6. "Our fundamentals are solid; it's just a matter of packaging." Another one of our favorites. It is simply amazing how many senior executives truly believe that the

problems in their organizations are simply a matter of packaging. If we can only tell the story right, if we can only list on the right stock exchange, if we can only have a more prestigious building, etc. Well, more often than not, it is not the packaging that is letting you down, it is the content. Your share price is not depressed because you are listed in the wrong market; it's depressed because your company has no financial vision and your investors see right through you. Your customers are not hanging up the phone because you do not have a catchy 800 number; they are hanging up because they wait forever to get a live person online. Never works!

We are sure by now that you know of the silver bullets we are talking about, and we can list a dozen more. As a new executive charged with making rapid and demonstrated change while fighting against the culture, expectations and time, it's critial that you identify these traps and steer clear of them.

<u>Rule #14: KISS – Keep it Simple and Short</u>

Your new team will likely have a dozen pet projects that they wish to accomplish for a variety of reasons. These projects will vary from large scope consultancies, silver bullet IT projects or the dreaded big bang white elephant projects which cost a bundle, take years to achieve (if ever) and occasionally end up in the corporate dustbin. Various employees adopt such projects for a variety of reasons, namely either politics, being sold on them by the consultant's spin, needing to beef up ones CV for future job prospects, or simply a lack of subject matter skills.

Examples of such corporate wide projects are massive ERP projects, data warehouses, document management solutions, process re-engineering, operations control systems, massive branding, CRM, etc. While we have nothing against such projects in the long term, unless they are professionally managed and carefully scoped, their chances of failure or delays are high, and their damage is doubled when the entire company waits patiently for these projects to end without implementing even small and practically cost-free incremental improvements.

On the other end of the spectrum, there are many value-added, pragmatic projects that can achieve relatively great improvements with little investment and risk. Examples are:

1. MIS: Companies often under-use their data and information assets because of the gaps in the user's ability to extract data and analyze it in an intuitive manner. Many companies that have not yet ventured into the world of data warehouses (with the costs and heartache that they impose) assume that the only way to get information from their systems is to repeatedly request reports and wait for an IT developer to build it, test it, and release it. Implementing focused data-marts for individual business units is a relatively low cost, quick, and high value project.

2. Project management: Project management skills are generally scarce in many companies. In addition, whatever skills do exist are often on a collision course with the vast majority of employees who neither practice nor understand PM standards, thus neutralizing existing skills. Simple awareness training sessions for concerned employees can go a long way toward achieving a unified

PM framework governing communications protocols and roles and responsibilities on high-risk projects.

3. IT Strategy: Dysfunction in the IT department can wreak havoc across the organization. Putting in place short- and long-term strategic plans aligned to corporate business goals is a high priority. This simple, short-term initiative can allow you to reap benefits in providing clearer IT plans, rationalizing resources and prioritization of key projects.

4. Intranets and Portals: These are very simple, cost-effective, and quick-to-implement ways to enhance corporate processes, communications and awareness. Workflow solutions today are easily implementable and can extend across the organization to reach employees through a variety of channels such as email and mobile devices.

5. Consultants: Consultants have always been viewed as the magic pill for all corporate ills. If you want to re-engineer processes, implement a change management program, a corporate reorganization, an ERP system or simply to get an subject matter expert in any of the myriad areas of knowledge that no employee has, the first quick answer is to get a consultant. Unfortunately, for every good consultant, there are ten bad ones, and another ten getting on-the-job training at your premises! Getting the right consultant is the first part of the battle (checking CV's, references, and calling them). The second part is agreeing on the correct scope of the engagement, and the final part is ensuring that the results are useable and that your employees acquired the skills to implement the consultant's deliverables.

Summary: Rules of the game constitute the operational framework and charter by which all stakeholders should abide to ensure effective synchronization of people, processes, systems and schedules. These rules involve agreeing on the various processes such as communication lines, reporting, escalations and project administrative functions and roles.

⌘　⌘　⌘

9. Low-Hanging Fruit

As we embark on our change mission and program, we need to remain aware of the short attention span and patience of Sponsors. If you refer to the opening chapters of this book and the "rah rah" message we get as the newcomers with a wide spreading mandate, delivery time of improvements will always be an issue to reckon with and manage carefully.

The most understanding and accommodating Sponsor who endorses an ambitious blueprint will recognize that change will require time. Yet, s/he they will soon run out of patience if changes are not evident quickly and ahead of schedule if possible. As a reader you might feel that we're generalizing and exaggerating, so we ask you to look back at your past record of successes and failures and honestly identify a time when a faster-than-planned change was adopted, and whether or not it resulted in goodwill and comfort for the sponsors.

These are what we refer to as the "low-hanging fruit". These are relatively low-effort / low-cost changes with high returns that can be identified and adopted rapidly and will help pave the way for the remainder of the blueprint. While you might not want to list them as core initiatives in your blueprint, always try to keep a ready supply of these wins. If you accumulate enough of them, they may form a core initiative of their own and transform into a major business enabler.

Low-hanging fruit will vary from one organization to another. In this chapter, we try to provide some insights about where to look for these wins and how to get the most mileage from seemingly small changes.

Start by looking at glaring process breakdowns. Are sales requests sitting in a queue (paper or electronic) way too long before they are processed and as a result, adversely affect sales targets? Can administrative processes be improved, i.e. are

An example of how to identify low-hanging fruit by going back to the basics is a transportation company we worked with that suffered from overstaffing, high cost base and inability to compete successfully with start-up competitors. A change program was created to examine the cost bases and slash costs where possible. Partly government-owned, the change mandate turned into a political nightmare with threats of strikes, and a total clamp down on working with the change team. This was a case where going back to the basics was a key factor in the change program, proceeding and delivering results. Rather than attack the problem from a work force reduction angle, the change team approached it from an increased efficiency angle, as well as instituting a team bonus structure. The basics of human nature that push us to compete and strive for monetary rewards were used. Going back to the basics, allowed the team to establish savings goals/targets for each department and then tasked the head of the department to achieve these targets without cutting the work force and set monetary rewards for the teams who achieve these goals. The results were amazing. After a slow start, the areas for savings started to be identified, and savings achieved. Then, the teams turned inward and started questioning some of their staffing levels and the cost of carrying some 'dead wood' in their groups, which were then identified and counseled out, Ultimately at the macro level, the organization started looking holistically at its functions and to areas where duplications and waste were evident and trimmed the fat. Machiavellian, probably, but it was the only way to get results going. Had the change team started cutting costs by laying people off the impact on the entire company would have been catastrophic.

leave requests taking too long to be approved, thus affecting employee morale? Is the process of scheduling meetings too time-consuming and a total waste of time? Are meetings themselves taking hours without providing closure to most issues? There will always be a supply of ideas and process breakdowns that can be fixed immediately, virtually cost-free and have a clear, quick, positive impact on the organization.

Another place to look for low hanging fruit are simple, quick and cost-free technology fixes. In this area, you need to be more careful, as technology projects have the tendency to grow exponentially from small changes into long and complex major projects. Are there forms that can be quickly turned into emails? Is there information that can be posted on the Intranet rather than passed around in paper form? Are there approvals that can flow over email? Are there simple tools that we can provide analysts with to reduce manual work and number crunching to generate reports that are more effective? Are collections and receivables not getting proper attention due to slow or inadequate exception reports from IT systems? Can a simple, consolidated pivot table or a simple business intelligence reporting system provide long sought after views on business performance? If the technology fixes cannot be done in less than 10 days at zero or little cost, then abandon them and look for another idea. Do not get trapped in endless 'IT' or departmental process re-engineering projects. This is not the time; you might need them to fulfill your blueprint and that is fine, but not as low hanging fruit. Remember the KISS principle.

A wealth of information that is usually overlooked is previous consulting work that was done. Most organizations have consultants' reports on their shelves that highlight areas of improvement. Sift through those reports and pick out the low-hanging fruit. Do not take full credit for identifying the improvement, but take credit for implementing it. This will also demonstrate the thoroughness of your work, as well as fiscal sense in not paying consultants to write the same report twice.

Similarly, prior internal audit reports can be collecting dust on a shelf yet may contain a wealth of unimplemented or delayed process compliance findings, new angles and supporting evidence on the same issues. Implementing these audit recommendations (i.e wins) can prove to have a triple benefit. First, the report findings are beneficial quick wins; secondly, they will improve the degree of compliance with internal audit recommendations, and thirdly, you may gain the internal audit function as an ally. Remember that consultants often use internal audit reports and either refer to them or present them in a new wrapper.

Ask around. In your meetings, preparation for the blueprint and debut presentation, as well as in building a change team, you should simply ask the question, "What can be done to immediately show results and improvements?" Make it your mantra. You will be surprised how insightful people can be when given an opportunity to be associated with a winning change program and when assured of credit once the improvements are carried out. As you are identifying and implementing these small but visible changes, keep the following in mind:

An example of why a change mandate needs to start showing results quickly and pluck all the low-hanging fruit is a large technology group within a global legal firm that, under the management of a new managing partner, was tasked with overhauling the entire technology infrastructure and support mechanism for the firm's offices around the globe. A new technology czar was hired and an ambitious 24-month blueprint was presented with great fanfare and approved, and precious funds were appropriated. More than a year into the program, the change team was on track with its blueprint and within its approved budget; great plans and foundations were being laid out. Yet, not a single meaningful win had been accomplished, as the head of the change program believed in 'big and substantial delivery'; an "all or nothing" approach was taken. Around this time, the law firm company merged with one of its rivals which had its own technology support group (we were their advisors), and as is typical of these deals, cost bases were examined and the large technology change program came under the scrutiny of the combined firm's senior partners. They demanded to know what results this program had yielded and were not pacified by long-term plans and promises of great wins that would take place in another year or so. As a result, the change team was disbanded, and a new mandate was issued with strict marching orders to deliver results immediately or face the risk of being outsourced. The planning and meticulous adherence to plans and budgets in the absence of quick wins could not save the change team nor salvage its mandate.

- This should not be an isolated phase of the change program. One of the common mistakes we make as CxOs is to start with a slew of easy wins, and then lose ourselves in the blueprint. There will always be low hanging fruit for us to pluck, and this should be an ongoing part of the process.

- Sometimes, you should just take the risk (it is contained anyway) and implement these improvements; do not worry about full approvals, lengthy discussions, etc.; just go for it. This will demonstrate the seriousness of your blueprint and change program as well a 'will-do' attitude that will roll out the change blueprint successfully.
- Keep track of these low hanging fruit, and celebrate the wins. There are no small changes, just changes that are not well packaged and presented or marketed.
- Update your blueprint with these wins and changes. You can include a category for 'additional improvements' that are above and beyond your change mandate.

Summary: Small changes can be as important as big, multi-stage, core changes. Identify these low-hanging fruit, deliver them quickly and celebrate their success visibly.

⌘　⌘　⌘

10. Momentum

With a good crop of low-hanging fruit plucked and showcased, a strong team in place and the culture of the organization understood and harnessed; now it is time for the big wins.

As we discussed earlier, the organizational attention and patience span for newcomers and CxOs is absurdly short, and the most understanding Sponsor will want results NOW. Starting with successes in the form of low-hanging fruit is useful but will only take your program so far.

At this point, your efforts should be to adhere religiously to the blueprint you have created and endorsed. Do not deviate and do not expand the scope (yet); your plan lays out the path forward.

When embarking on your debut large ticket item, the following can help increase your chances of success and mitigate the initial risks that are typical of large change programs:

- Plan the program/initiative very carefully and create a formal presentation (to be shared with and approved by the sponsor first). This will introduce the initiative and explain how it fits into and supports the change blueprint, and what the various stakeholders and affected organizational units or processes should expect. For example, if your first initiative is a review of the company's procurement practices to identify process breakdowns and potential savings, you need to involve all the affected areas such as inventory and warehousing, accounting, technical staff, etc. and get them on your side from day one. You also need to sell the ideas to the affected departments or groups whose normal procurement flow may be affected as you overhaul this function. Just because it was listed and explained in the blueprint does not mean it was fully understood or fully accepted, nor viewed as an upcoming reality. Communicate repeatedly.

- Be realistic in your timeframes and end results; fight the impulse to shorten the required timeframes to impress the group with how fast you can deliver results ahead of schedule, and below budget. Rest assured that your peers and sponsors assign more importance to achieving meaningful results than to sticking to an aggressive schedule at the cost of quality or simply to achieve flashy but superficial results.

- Stay focused and do not stray from the original goals of this initiative. Again, once you get rolling, the temptation will be to load up more and more on the original scope (the infamous "scope creep" syndrome). If you do not maintain strong self-discipline you might achieve some additional wins, but you greatly risk losing ground on your original mandate for the sake of peripheral tasks that should come later.

- Communicate your progress, issues and risks repeatedly as you still have not built the ideal comfort level of your sponsors and the organization. You need to communicate as frequently as you can without boring them to death. Do review the project details behind the scenes, but avoid minutia during meetings, and do take the time to communicate major progress milestones, issues, and risks, while keeping in mind that you can always scale back in later stages when you have reached a higher level of comfort and trust.

- Most importantly, finish the job on time, on budget and deliver ALL your goals and tasks, without shortcuts, and without sweeping thorny issues under the rug.

Rinse and repeat! Until you are done with your blueprint.

It is also important to keep track of your progress on these large-scale initiatives and to continually update the blueprint. A good practice is to present the updated project plan weekly and the updated blueprint monthly. You need to keep reinforcing and reminding your audience about how the larger-scale change program is progressing and how and where this facilitating cog fits in the wheel.

Celebrate the completion of your first large project with even more fanfare. Reward your team members, gloat if you can and highlight the credibility of your blueprint. Then turn your attention and energy to the next big project and repeat the cycle.

When it comes to these large-scale, multi-faceted change blueprints, there is no escaping the basics and fundamentals. The work must be done and given its due time and labor. Do not get distracted by success or boredom; do not become complacent and do not lower your guard. You still have a long way to go.

Nevertheless, as we discuss the plan for the big wins, we also need to anticipate, accept and recover from the failures. In the perfect business world that we all dream of, projects proceed according to plan, peers are supportive, sponsors are decisive, budgets materialize on time and team members never leave us. Until we are there, we need to be prepared for missed deadlines, reduced budgets, scope changes, sudden new risks, employee turnover, overt and covert resistance, and in some cases, failed projects.

An example of a company that could not get the momentum of change going is a large developer of luxury properties that we worked with that initiated a large-scale change program to elevate the company to a higher class in the market. With all the right pieces in place, the company suffered from a chronic reluctance to maintain a rhythm, partly driven by a leadership that is used to quick and small projects, but it was also attributed to a lack of blueprint that can harness this energy and direct it in a consistent manner towards a longer term goal. When working with this organization, we spent an inordinate amount of time on the blueprint and agreed on ambitious goals, and then used the small achievements as building blocks towards the ultimate goal. This helped created congruity between the achievements, as well as demonstrating to the organization how all the pieces can fit together, without forcibly changing the culture of the organization. What would normally be broken down into 4-6 large projects was turned into 20+ small tasks that helped create a sense of accomplishment and built on the strength of the organization

We never embark on a project or change initiative with the expectation that it will fail, but it would be naive not to put controls, precautions and the proverbial "Plan B" in place in the unfortunate event that we do experience a partial or full initiative failure.

As CxOs and new executives, we will need to dig deep and regroup; in addition, we need to be honest with our sponsors on why this particular project, initiative, or change goal failed to reach its mark, and what work-arounds and secondary plans need to be enacted.

Was it the planning, the timeframe, the culture, the timing or all of the above? As highly effective and accomplished professionals, it bruises our egos and creates webs of doubt in our heads when we experience a failure of this sort. This is not the time to panic nor should we start doubting our own abilities. This is the time for regrouping, going back to the basics and then, preparing for a re-launch.

Summary: As the designated CxO, you want to be known as a delivery resource. You are not a theorist. You implement workable, lasting solutions. The organization has probably gone through scores of consultants and "visionaries", and now they desperately need to see real change. Your first big win, your "home run", will blaze your trails for you as you go through your blueprint. However, prepare for hiccups along the way, and be resilient in your recovery.

⌘　⌘　⌘

11. Templates and Forms – Building a routine

A good part of the successful CxO's tool kit is a set of forms and templates that can be easily deployed at the onset of a blueprint implementation process.

While the reader may wonder about the value that a set of templates can add to a large-scale, ambitious change program, in many cases these tools and templates can have a lasting effect on the entire organization and how it operates. The value is both tangible and qualitative, spanning the following benefits:

- It helps the CxO introduce changes that are key to the success of the blueprint. These forms and templates can help fix broken processes, and give new life to old, tired ones. As we discussed in the "Back to Basics" chapter, going to the basics is a key ingredient in achieving the goals of any change program.
- These forms and templates also signal the start of a new era of change and a demonstrated departure of old practices. They are also an easy win and a source of low-hanging fruit that the CxO can draw on rather easily and quickly. These forms and templates are, for the most part, free, quick and far-reaching. From our experiences, we found that a simple form or template that can be polished up, customized and adopted in a matter of days if not hours can have more impact than a drawn-out expensive IT project.

- The forms and templates are also good ways to break the ice with various departments, functions and teams so as to understand what they do and inject a healthy dose of change without running the risk of 'This is how we used to do it' that we discussed earlier.
  Forms need not necessarily be paper-based. Today's email and Office automation software (MS office, Domino, etc.) can achieve even more benefits and efficiencies in the same timeframe needed to design the forms but without the paper waste and inefficiencies. Just do not let such projects take on a life of their own and mushroom into full-blown IT programs.

So what forms and templates are we talking about? Examples:

- <u>Meeting agenda and minutes</u>. While the reader might again wonder if there are organizations out there that still do not adopt these basic meeting best practices, from our consulting experience, we can safely say YES. If you take a good, hard, objective look at the tools your organization has, chances are you will find them to be outdated, cumbersome to use and rarely used at all. Polished electronic versions of meeting agendas and minutes can spruce up some of the dull meetings that go on forever and rarely result in tangible results.
- <u>Project/initiative/KPI tracking and progress reports</u>. One of our pet peeves. It is staggering how many major initiatives and projects are run based on word-processors, excel sheets and informal or extremely complex (but

misused) project management tools. The tool itself is irrelevant if it is not being applied and used. As you are trying to understand the lay of the land, introduce simple-to-follow, easy project tracking and progress reports. This will help you assess the quality of the project management skills of your stakeholders; it will also help your team get a consistent bird's-eye view of what is happening in the field. Key Performance Indicators (KPI's) can be simplified into measurable and repeatable periodic reports that can instill a sense of competitiveness and achievement on a periodic basis.

- Financial tracking sheets and Analytical Pivot tables. Forget detailed budgets and endless ledgers of revenue and expenses. What we are talking about is introducing simple financial tracking sheets that can help bring up to the surface the underlying financial elements of broken processes, baselines, delayed projects and more importantly, successes.

- Inter-divisional forms. Examples could be purchase order forms for frequently purchased/delayed items or to facilitate another division's processes. The forms should be agreed upon in a collaborative process where the other division does not perceive this as stepping on their turf. Such forms spread the message of change beyond your division's boundaries and send a positive signal of a collaborative win-win approach.

As long as these tracking sheets are not perceived as an evaluation or assessment of the owner or end by themselves, they can be very useful and a great source of easy wins and a push for more change.

Whether these forms should be automated, or paper based; where they are stored and shared is not the point of this chapter. We are also sure the reader can identify many other forms that can be introduced easily and profitably. The simple criteria to follow are:

- Can this form/template be understood and implemented in days?
- Is it free/low-cost and easy to implement?
- Does it introduce a new best practice or fix a broken one quickly?

Naturally, you can expect resistance to surface for several reasons and from various groups:

- "We already have this form/template and it never worked," or "What we have is much better and simpler."
- "We already have too many things to do and don't need the extra red tape."
- "This is irrelevant to our culture."

And the list can go on and on.

Our advice to you CxOs is to be firm in the implementation of these practices. Your goal is to introduce change, break the logjam and get the right energy going. Manage the resistance tactfully but firmly. Once the routine starts to set in place and the new way of doing things takes hold, change will follow. At the same time, be realistic, remember the KISS rule and adhere to it as much as you can. Another good trick is to have your team members or even better, the stakeholders, champion some of these new practices. They become owners and advocates for the new order. At the same time, do not fall into the trap of the consultant who has a magical bag of tricks and expects them to work everywhere and with every audience. You will need to spend some time and effort to customize and adapt them to the culture in which you now find yourself.

Summary: Introducing new forms/templates and standardized practices helps the CxO bring about useful, easy, quick and demonstrable changes. Keep it simple, and manage the resistance.

12. The Wind-Down

Coming from practical experience, getting a major initiative or project wrapped up and closed can be as challenging and taxing as it was to get it launched.

A change blueprint should clearly highlight the wind-down and wrap-up protocols and set clear steps to commence the wind-down process of change tasks, and at the macro level, the entire change blueprint.

As you move down your change path and deliver on your change mandates, it is necessary to clearly plan the closure steps; however, it is also important to <u>avoid some common traps</u>:

1. <u>Change is perpetual and cannot be stopped.</u> While it is true that we operate in an environment of constant change, the change program and blueprint should have a discrete timeframe and deliverables that signify the completion of one stage and the beginning of another.

2. <u>Let's take the change blueprint and morph it into change blueprint stage II, III,</u> etc. Again, while this is a testament to the success of your first blueprint and an affirmation of the value of the change blueprint, it is a very risky practice. Unless you establish clear demarcation lines between each successive change blueprint and subsequent mandate, you will end up with programs that bleed into each other and will likely result in a never-ending cycle. This also implies lost opportunities to effectively implement change and to display the successes of your initial blueprint.

3. <u>Let's turn the change program into a corporate function.</u> This has to be one of the most absurd approaches

to implementing change, yet sadly, we see it more often than expected. Building on the success of the change blueprint and the initial delivery of projects and home runs, the sponsors have an automatic reaction to turn this change initiative into another corporate function or department. In their minds, in order to embed change in the fabric or DNA of the organization, this is required. Fancy names are given to these units, like "Perpetual Development", "Process Optimization", "Special Projects" and others that will only serve to turn an energized change team and change blueprint into just another bureaucratic corporate function, struggling with the same baggage and limitations of the organization. What sponsors fail to recognize is that a great deal of the credibility and success of the change team, agent and blueprint stems from the fact that it's set up as a task force with a clear but different mandate and a finite timeframe. Rather than killing the spirit of change and risking the loss of all the hard-won gains, change blueprints should be allowed to operate as originally planned, and when the blueprints are delivered, new blueprints and change initiatives can emerge. Nevertheless, never as a corporate function.

4. <u>Let's freeze all future change initiatives for x months until the blueprint shows results</u>. This is a fast track to disaster. In essence, this sends the message to the organization that while we endorsed the change and worked hard to implement its goals, let us now sit back, reflect and assess it to death. What will invariably happen is that energy will dissipate, focus will be lost and old practices and broken processes will reemerge stronger than

ever. Thus, the prospect of future change blueprints is doomed. Yes, change initiatives should be assessed, and yes, they should be given time to burn in, but do not freeze change. At the one extreme, organizations want to stay in a perpetual state of change; at the other, they want to freeze change. Both are dangerous. Many change programs and blueprints have been written off and dropped AFTER delivering their intended results because organizations did not know what to do next!

An example of why a change mandate needs to have established and agreed wind-down procedures and demarcation lines comes from a start-up company we worked with during the .com era on the West Coast. The company was suffering from growing pains that are typical of all start-up operations when things get out of hand faster than anyone can anticipate. We were called in as part of a large consulting team to get the company on track and build an institution from what in essence was a group of bright people all doing their own thing at their own pace. A comprehensive plan was designed and agreed, and we attacked the problems from many sides, i.e. sales, marketing, finance, operations, etc. as well as structure, strategy, and the like. What we failed to recognize at the time was that, unlike established companies, the lines between these functions were not only blurry, they simply didn't exist, and within weeks of the great Champagne kickoff we found ourselves in a situation that can only be described as a swamp of changes occurring at all the levels of the organization without any discernible beginnings or ends. The chaotic nature of the business itself only added to the problem, and what was interesting was that we recognized the problem before the client did. We ended up drawing clear lines between the change events and a more managed sequence of change that takes in account the nature of the company and its capabilities.

As CxOs, we need to practice our skills and deploy them on the wrap-up of our blueprints with the same energy and zeal we have shown on the launch and delivery of our mandates. A few tricks of the trade to help in this arena:

A. Institute a formal closure process for each initiative under your change blueprint, and secure a formal set of acceptance and closure criteria against the original goals.

B. Constantly update your blueprint with completed change elements, and publish their progress. Show the remaining work against the original mandate.

C. Resist the urge to substitute one change element with another to assuage pressures from sponsors or function owners. A carefully crafted, planned and orchestrated blueprint is built on inter-dependencies and a carefully scheduled sequence of events. While exchanging one change element for another can work, it may raise the risk profile of the entire blueprint. If you are faced with tremendous pressure to accelerate one element or swap it with new ones, handle with utmost care and highlight boldly on your progress reports.

D. Identify and capture genuine and talented new CxOs. This area can be tackled after you deliver on your original mandate, either under the umbrella of a new change blueprint or as follow-up work. This should be approached with the same diligence and given the same attention as the blueprint was. Another good practice is to farm them out to other corporate functions as ambassadors of change and as auxiliary CxOs.

Summary: We like to see logical beginnings and ends. There is nothing more satisfying than seeing completed progress reports and tasks ticked off our change mandate. If you have ever added a task to your to-do list and turned around to tick it off minutes later, you know what we are talking about. The closure of the blueprint and its underlying tasks is as critical as the work that goes into the planning and execution.

⌘   ⌘   ⌘

www.ingramcontent.com/pod-product-compliance
Lightning Source LLC
Chambersburg PA
CBHW071722170526
45165CB00005B/2110